THE SCARY ABECEDARY
(A Horror Poetry Alphabet Book)

Brooke MacKenzie

THE SCARY ABECEDARY
(A Horror Poetry Alphabet Book)

CURVED QUILL PRESS

PRAISE FOR THE SCARY ABECEDARY:

"With 26 poems teased from skin and tissue and veiny threads, Brooke MacKenzie's *The Scary Abecedary* resounds with brutality, fragility, and fear. A startling debut and a lesson for our times." —Lee Murray, five-time Bram Stoker Award®-winner and author of *Tortured Willows*

"A nightmare for every letter. Sincere and spined, MacKenzie's abecedary is a worthy primer in the unflinching language of dark prose." –Lindy Ryan, Bram Stoker Award®-nominated editor of *Into the Forest*

"The alphabet in The Scary Abecedary is both of this world and beyond it, spelling out historical terrors, supernatural terrors, psychological terrors, and terrors very much grounded in the political here and now…Brooke MacKenzie has given us a primer like no other, chilling and cathartic." –Gayle Brandeis, author of *Many Restless Concerns*, nominated for the Shirley Jackson Award

For my mother, Janet McCaffrey

*Thank you for always encouraging my poetry,
even when the smell of the scented candles and
incense that I liked to burn while writing
was almost unbearable*

Introduction

Abecedary [ey-bee-see-*duh*-ree] : The alphabet, written out
in a teaching book, or carved on a wall; a primer

There are so many frightening things
And in imposing an alphabetic structure onto them,
I am attempting to control and contain them
It is a futile effort to make everything seem less
scary

Each letter of the alphabet has been assigned a
fright
Sometimes the poems are scary, sometimes they're
gruesome, sometimes subversive,
Sometimes deeply personal

Because the definition of "scary" shifts and changes
depending upon
The layers of feelings and experiences and moods
That cover our eyes like a film

Our lenses shift and our pupils dilate and our minds
go along for the ride

But there are so many frightening things

And they seem to multiply with each passing day….

Will we ever be safe again?

Were we ever really safe at all?

WELCOME

You are afraid to go into your own house
Afraid to hear the click-clacking soundtrack
Of the mechanized noises that fill the walls
Drumming like filthy fingernails from a
disembodied spirit
The conductor of your anxious orchestra

You are afraid to go into your own house
With its debris and detritus
Coating the floor like layers of mica
As you peel them off,
You peel your own skin

You are afraid to go into your own house
As the day's whispers, encounters, conflicts
Follow you inside and become trapped there
And they are whipped up into a frenzied orbit
Around your head
Repeating themselves, repeating themselves,
Repeating themselves
Their words create angry shapes
Behind your eyelids
Until you can no longer close them

You are afraid to go into your own house
And enter it the way the mites enter your skin
The living things you can't see
Inhabit your
Hair and eyes and teeth and lips and viscera
And you swear you can hear them nibbling

And, no, the bleach doesn't reach them
And when you try to put your head on the pillow
You think you can hear them talking on its surface
Saying moist, mucous-filled words
That pop like spit bubbles

You are afraid to go into your own house
Because you can feel your frailty becoming more
pervasive
Your body robs you from the inside out
Making your bones hollow
Your breath elusive
Your mind gelatinous
And each hour that passes within those walls
Dissolves you just a little more
You are becoming a crusty membrane
With nothing underneath
One day you will simply crumble
Like a withered autumn leaf
And be swept away
To make space for someone else's season

You are afraid to go into your own house
To see its walls covered in images of your regrets
Like wallpaper, like faded photographs
It is haunted with the memories of moments
When you didn't know that the feeling
Knitting up your insides
Was contentment
Or even joy
You hear the ghost of your own laughter

A noise that is now shrill and unfamiliar
As you darken your senses with solitude

There is nowhere else to go
You step onto the mat
That spreads its greeting
Like a rotting smile

Welcome home.

B is for Black Dahlia

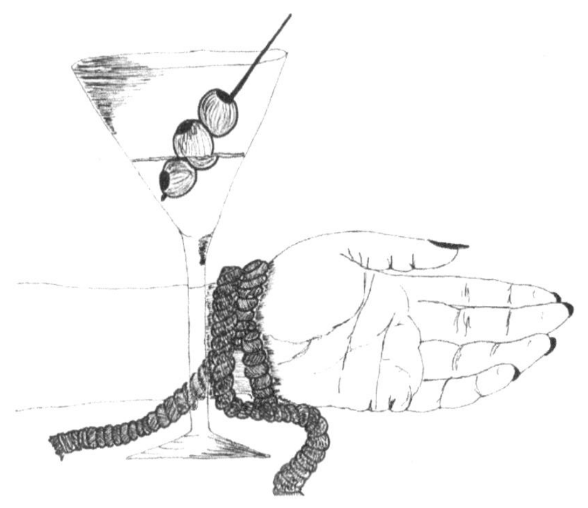

No one knows the whole story. They never will.

All they know is the aftermath. The way you sliced
and diced my body
Julienned my intestines
Drained me of fluids and blood
And the clotted mess of your semen
And, because you loved my smile
You carved my face like a petal pink Jack-O'-
Lantern
So that when they finally did find me
My garish grin would be the standout feature

You first noticed my smile in that hotel bar that was
just a shade too dark
And the voluptuous tones of the jazz music were
just a shade too loud
And so I couldn't even draw you in
With the salty sultriness of my voice because
I had to shout so you could hear me over the
trumpet,
Its shape like the martini glass I eyed you over
The drink had been perfect in its balanced dirtiness
And its ice chips were like tiny rhinestones

That was only the beginning.

I'm married, you had said
I simply put my finger to my lips
Right where you would put your lips later
And every night for the next month

My heart flickered like that broken streetlight on the
corner
Where you slipped your arms around my waist and
pulled me into you
And I fell like a stone into a wishing well
Not even bothering to create ripples on that dark,
fetid water
I never found the bottom

No, not never. The bottom came eventually.
The final dilation of my pupils before that last
Shuddering breath

But that would come later.

First, the hissing tendrils of your whispered
confessions
Would get tangled in my hair
Absorbed by my ears
And so
When you said that we should go to your office
To be alone
No other word than "yes" could make its way
To the front of my mouth
And spill out like melted butter

Your office was in the basement
A sterile space in an equally sterile building
I shivered when I entered it
The instruments were pristine and freezing
Tools for healing your many patients
You lifted me onto the examination table

Your tongue doing its own examination of my
mouth
While my thighs spread
Cradling your hip bones
Your hands were eager butterflies
Almost hovering above my skin
Making all of the fleshy parts of me swell and
sweeten,
Waiting.

When your hands reached my wrists
There was an unexpected pressure and I yelped
Your eyes had disappeared behind
A scrim of rage
And your lips had thinned
Into a sneer
The ropes were hungry snakes
And they wound their way around my joints all too
easily
Digging into my skin with their venomous fangs

The hours were numerous
Marching slowly like wounded soldiers
Blindly following commands

You began feeding me
Stuffing me full of the unimaginable:
Cockroaches, my own waste, a searing acid

You waved your scalpel like a conductor's wand
Orchestrating a symphony of torture
That left an indelible mark on that basement room
And it would forever seep into your future patients

In spite of your uncanny ability to keep everything
Clean clean clean
Pristine

You carved your marks all over my skin
And in the dark parts of my mind
The parts beyond the frantic, animalistic reach
Of fight or flight
I couldn't shake the sadness

I had loved you
I had wanted every part of you
With every inch of my truly wasted flesh
And even as you severed my spine after my death
Sawing slowly, rhythmically
The hollow sound of it
Finding its way to wherever you had deposited my
soul
You were not able to rid me of that love
You were not able to empty it the way you did
The rest of my inner streams
And internal pockets

They will never write about that
About my desires
The hope that you would whisk me away
From the filthy parts of that hopeless city
I would have been your secret forever
Wrapped in your love like a gift

Instead their ink spilled and splattered
Far messier than my blood had been
With descriptions of the body you dumped

That had been scrubbed clean of my own gore

They would call me a prostitute
A party girl
A desperate ingenue, having finally found
The grisly stardom I sought
In those twinkling hills

But, in the end, I had been a person.
A woman, waiting to be loved
To be rescued
To belong to someone.

C is for Creek

It was payday for the laborers from China.

The ones whose backs were stooped with the hunt
for gold
As they picked and dug and scooped out a hostile
earth
The ones whose tongues tangled around silky
syllables
That jarred the wealthy white ears of the mine
owners

The laborers gathered where they were told
After being rounded up like cattle
By the men on horseback

The laborers waited, their hands clasped, ready
For them to be filled with money
A pittance, really, but a life-sustaining one
Enough to allow their spines to rest and
Their stomachs to quiet their clamoring

There was nothing in China for them
Not any longer
Just the bareboned heat of violence and desperation
And so
They gathered, collectively quiet
Waiting in this steep cavern by a winding creek
In a place far more beautiful than any one place
deserved to be

The mine owner appeared
Joined by ten of his men
Tipping a buckskin cowboy hat and a grin

With teeth like pieces of crooked quartz
The same kind of rock that traces like a vein to the
motherlode
The men wore matching smirks
Soft slashes across their faces
Their eyes glinting like gold flecks in the
Misguided river

And then
There was a silver flash
As ten machetes were raised in unison
Over ten heads
But just for an instant
Before they were lowered into
Necks chests heads
The whooshing sound of the blade slicing the air
Ended in a wet thud as it hit flesh and bone
Shrieks and groans splattered against
The walls of the cavern as the laborers
Strained to escape
Bodies fell into the creek
Sheets of red covered them like funeral shrouds
Blood stained the rocks, stained the water
Stained that piece of earth forever

When the very last gasp
Bubbled up from the very last throat
And the last artery
Spurted its last offering
The mine owner gathered his men
Like a child tidying up playthings
And let the creek do their cleanup
Their hands and pockets bulging and bloated

With money
With murder
With greed

And now
Today
And every single day
Kids fish here
In this stained creek
They fish here
At Bloody Run Creek
A name that has lost its potency
With generations of innocuous repetition
A name dropped easily into the same sentence as
Summer and *weekend*

Today
It is just a creek in a cavern
In a place far more beautiful than any one place
deserves to be

D is for Doppelganger

Each of us has a doppelganger
A splintered off piece of our own mythology
The dark sliver of our soul
Wrapped in a blanket of flesh
Designed to match our own

The doppelgangers
Wander a misty mountain landscape
One that is simultaneously jagged and wet
That exists on the edge of our reality
Framing it, containing it
The same way the shapes of our ocular bones
Hold our eyes in place

The doppelgangers
Wait and watch until the time is right
And then, like an eyeball popping out of place
They burst the membrane between their world and
ours
Spilling their darkness
Like the thin liquid that dribbles out of blisters, out
of wounds
Assuming our identities
And inserting their dark figures into our
Incomplete brightness

The doppelgangers
Do their deeds
In their undiminished hatred
And then
Travel through this earthen landscape
Loving soil, loving air
Acting out the worst parts of ourselves

Collecting our
Raging vengeful hateful parts
And carrying them in the veiny container
Of their slightly translucent bodies

The doppelgangers
Carry these things so that we do not have to
We can move forward in goodness
Relieved of evil
Dutiful and beautiful
While they strike the ground
Our dark angels, our forgotten twins
Heavy with our sins
So that we may be light

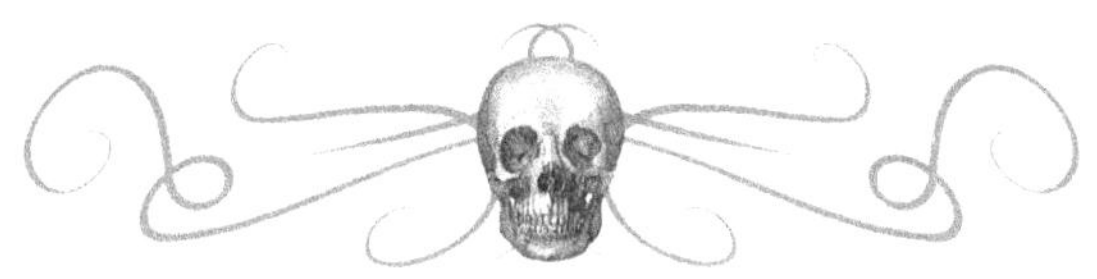

E is for Eternity/Exit/Expectations/Ending

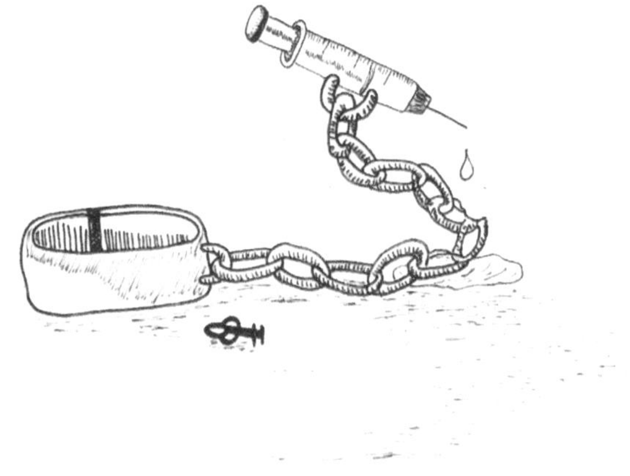

What is it that keeps you here?
Who are you waiting for?
I have heard your footsteps pacing relentlessly
In the empty bedroom above mine
Circling, circling, circling through your own stuck
surfaces
Waiting for someone to come home
Someone who never will
Someone who waits for you elsewhere

Smoke and hope and loneliness
Constitute your being like vapors
Inconsequential and immaterial
Because you should no longer be here
But your own expectations tether you
To a life that no longer wants you
To a place with new tenants who
Trudge through their own routines—
The mechanized minutes
The yawning hours
The blurry weeks and waterfall months
Not realizing that it will all end.

But it will.
And it does.
And still,
An ending is a greater gift than an eternity
Of waiting and pacing.

Go.

F is for Fire

There is a witch inside of me
That I constantly try to burn
Purify with fire
Even as she sings her wisdom
Through a throat full of smoke

Her smoldering truths fill my organs
My heart
And still, I coat her words in flames
Swallowing their orange spears like little tongues

My insides turn crisp and curl like ancient papers
My blood becomes thick and immobile
My eyes cloud and darken
And my tongue bursts, stopping speech

Burn the witch
Burn the witch
Burn the witch down

But she refuses to become ash
The flames sculpt her bones
Making them malleable
She can bend and flex and fit herself
Into the spaces where the fire can't go
The corners of my body, my brain
That are still light and lavender

And the witch whispers
Her incantations and evocations and provocations
Until my internal inferno
Becomes an ember
Twinkling in my innards

Resting until my next rage

Burn the witch
Burn the witch
Burn the witch down

But the witch will remain
Fed and fortified by fire
Speaking and teaching
Reaching out to me
Even as I am engulfed in my own arson

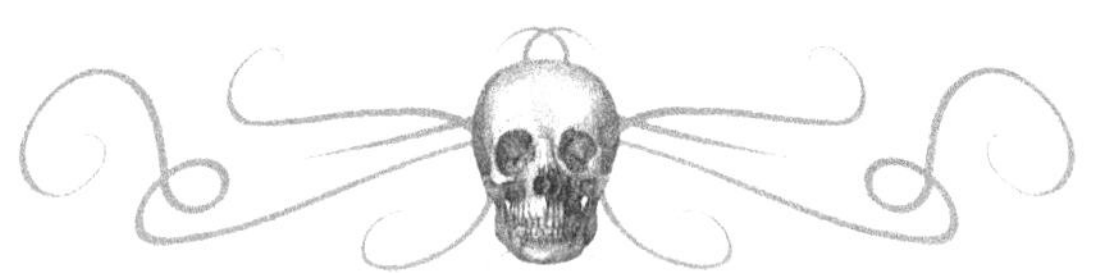

G is for Ghosts

Spooky ghosts and
Howling ghosts and
Tortured ghosts right here,
Making all their noises in the darkness of your ear

Creeping ghosts and
Singing ghosts and
There's a happy one,
Floating all around your head after the day is done

They haunt your dreams
Infect your schemes
And sneak up from behind,
They pull your nerves like strings
'Til they have tangled up your mind

So don't let them inside your house
And not inside your head,
They're lonely and they will not rest
Until you're like them: DEAD

H is for Her Horses

Her horses
Are revved up by the light of the full moon as they
stamp the ground, making semicircle shapes like
tiny pelvises, and the edges of their hooves puncture
the ground like bursting wombs

Her horses
Smell vulnerability on that dank autumn breeze,
their nostrils wide like the terrible, terrible full
moon and quivering like silent violin strings until a
burst of their aggressive breath vibrates into a snort,
into the sound of pigs and earth demons and
creatures far baser than horses are meant to be

Her horses
Plow their way out of the barn, metal scraping
wood, horseshoes scraping pavement, massive
bones scraping the underside of their hides as their
legs build up speed and beat the landscape into
submission

Her horses
Are sleek, dark arrows, compressing space and
distance into a singular target: a human bullseye
astride a quiet horse—one that would never join
their chase—and Quiet Horse and Rider make a
unified, relaxed silhouette in the light of the terrible,
terrible full moon. And then, the shapes are
separated as a starving snout knocks Rider from
Quiet Horse, sending Quiet Horse into a flurry of
instinct as it gallops away, while Rider writhes in
surprise. There is no time for an injury inventory
because

Her horses
Have bitten into Rider's ribcage and flung it open
with the same arcing neck motion that they use to
tear stubborn grasses from the ground. The chorus
of snorts rises up again under that terrible, terrible
full moon as dull white teeth dive into an open chest

Her horses
Feast on variety meats: lungs and arteries and tissue
while blood and fur make a lacquer that splatters
across legs and the ground. Rider's heart is saved
for the strongest, fastest horse and its head rises and
falls, serpentine and striking, devouring the heart
with a bulbous swallow

Her horses
Once sated, lick themselves with sloppy tongues
and gnaw gently at each other's withers. Grooming,
tending, and nuzzling as the terrible, terrible full
moon is gulped down by the horizon. They wander
slowly home, sweetening their mouths with grass as
their stomachs roil with meat and roughage and
their cravings are tamped back down into a
leisurely, droning background sound

Her horses
Will now be dormant, obedient—delightful, even—
until the next terrible, terrible full moon.

I is for Insomnia

I can't sleep on account of the bubbles in my brain
stem

They travel up and down that narrow chamber,
bulging because
there's not enough room for them
and so they threaten to burst and make me bleed out

The bubbles are shaped by dread and memories

Floating up, bouncing against my brain and
dropping back down again, making my head itch
from the inside

And the bubbles make a tick-tick-ticking sound in
time with the clock

Counting down the restless seconds of time passing
with no sleep

The memories the bubbles produce are
Neutered skeletons that creak and clack and taunt
but have no substance

It's the worry for the future that turns beastly in that
chemical bath of sleeplessness,
growling out the worst case scenarios

The worry taps its pointed fingernails against its
even more pointed teeth, a monstrous metronome

Reminding me that the cord of control I have wound
around the pieces and people of my life is utterly
invisible, unable to be grasped

The only thing I am really holding is my own fist

My fingernails leave hungry smiles in the heel of
my palm

The bubbles tick and the beast becomes more
beastly and sleep is more elusive and
there's nothing I can do

J is for Jersey Devil

I saw it once

Its wings were spread so wide
They darkened an entire patch of sky
Absorbing all light and color
And its scarlet eyes were almost beautiful
Rubies quivering with malicious intent
Its jaws opened
Solid enough to grind bones into dust

And its ear-melting shriek saturated the air
Rattling my teeth and the tiny shapes in my ears
It was many different pitches threaded together
In a noose of noise
All I could do was cover my ears and scream back

The two of us were wounded creatures
Boiling in our own pain
Letting the endless steam of it escape through our
mouths
Crescendoing into an unbearable sound

And with a cataclysmic flap of its wings, it was
gone
Out of my sight
Out of the world
For a little while, at least
Leaving a vacuum that sucked at my chest

I wish I could say that the silence was peaceful
But instead it stung
The way skin feels in the aftermath of a slap

I was left alone with myself
Once again
But still,
I keep my eyes forever skyward, scanning
For a creature that is far less frightening
Than my own thoughts.

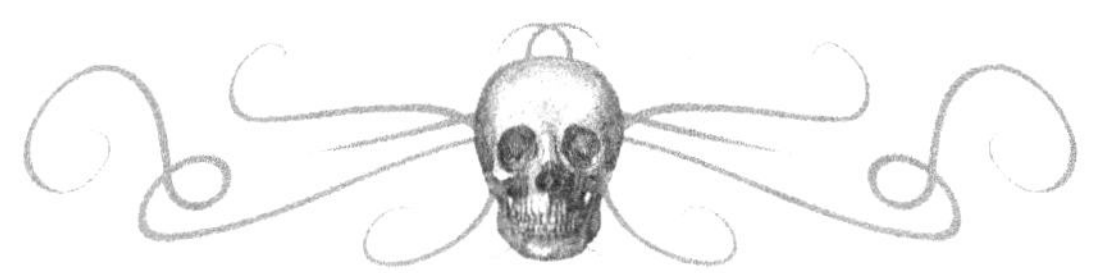

K is for Kissing Beetles (A Painful Ode To an Unfortunate Allergy)

Such an innocuous name, delightfully so
They get it from their proclivity to bite faces
Digging their snouts deep into the satin patch of an
eyelid
Or a cheek as it blushes in sleep,
Leaving watery lumps behind as a morning surprise
And they make my entire body blossom into hives
Sprinkling that pollinated itch over my eyes and lips
and tongue
And when that happens
Air becomes scarce
And liquid luck in the shape of a needle
Is the only salvation
For that unwelcome penetration

Their bites make me breathless
At night I feel the beetles crawling under my skin
Scuttling across the fibers of my nerves
The mucus membranes of my skeletal system
Making toxic shapes in my limbs as they crawl and
zigzag,
Thick with chemical curiosity
Their little feet stinging with each step on the inside
of my body where there is no relief
I think they might be in the couch
Or under the blanket as I battle my insomnia with
the visual balm of television
But they're in me and so I start
Scratching, scratching, scratching
My fingernails can't reach
And the click clack clackety sound of their crawling
Echoes in the hollows of my bones and in the meaty
space at the back of my jaw

And then the beetles find their way to my optic
nerves
Where they tug and twist, master puppeteers
Forcing my eyelids open and my corneas to turn dry
And the bulge in my vision makes everything look
convex
And the boiling blisters bubble up from a lower
layer of my skin
Making my body crimson and my heart a deep plum
purple
As it pumps air through swelling passages
And I thrash and scratch and scream and slowly fill
with fluid
Drowning in my own body until finally,
Unsheathing my own EpiPen Excalibur,
I stab my villainous self in the thigh

The passageways open and the beetles disappear
into puffs of smoke
Snaking out through my nostrils and my body
heaves into breath
Tonight these unlikely foes have been vanquished
But they will be back
Too tempting is my taut skin and all my threaded
fibers
The mincemeat parts of me.

L is for Locket

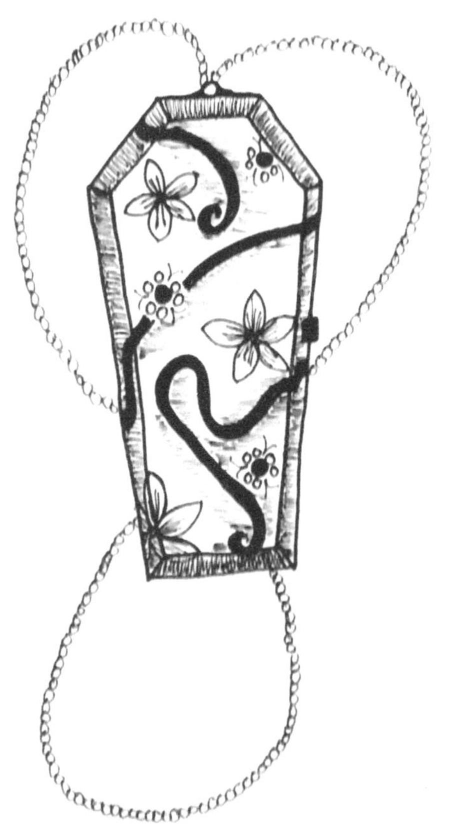

A coffin opens

The air escapes, brushing the cheeks

     of loved ones like handkerchiefs

A precious keepsake tucked inside

Forever perfect

     a final snapshot for memory

A coffin closes

     and is nestled into the earth

The way a necklace nestles

     between a sweater and a beating heart

It is death's locket.

M is for The Missing

54

What happens to the missing?

To the girls whose bones whistle and sing
In an unknown wind? Whose skeletons are
Bleached or broken or damp or dissolving
Depending upon where they end up?

What happens to the screams that never had a
chance
To land in the ears of their salvation?

What happens to the dreams that filled
The hollows of their chests,
Before the air was crushed out of them?

Their teeth are the last things to disappear
And they chomp at the earth and air
Trying to speak
Even though the rest of them has dried up
And become a simple tapestry of cells
Indistinguishable from their surroundings
Wherever they may be

But their teeth clatter and gnash and carve the air

They try to tell us about those
Final seconds
About those last few beats
Before violence swooshed its cape
And walked away the victor

Our ears are not tuned to the frequency of teeth
And so, we continue to ask…..

What happens to the missing?

The teeth know. Look there.

56

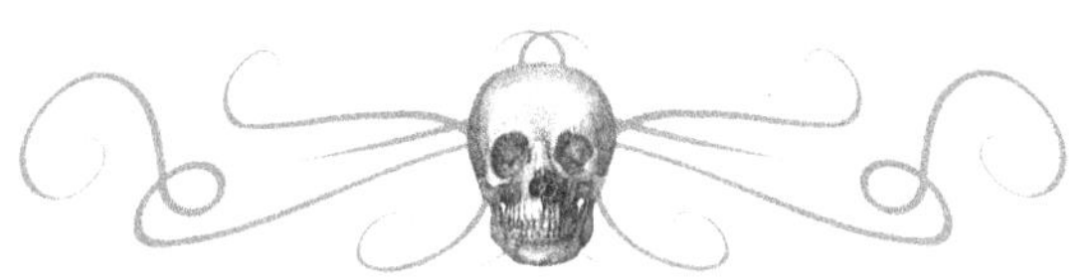

N is for Night Stalker (Richard Ramirez)

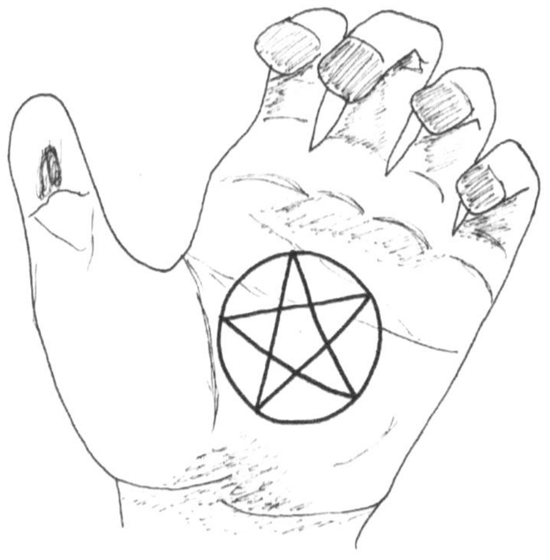

Sometimes I think that I see you
Out of the corner of my eye
Staring at me through those evil chasms in your
skull
Holding up your branded palm like a folded,
withered leaf
HAIL SATAN

But I think the Prince of Darkness cast you out
You are unwanted, even by the hell fires that left
you
Scalded, blistered, oozing
Your managed darkness extinguished them
Turning them to ash and smoke

And so you drift
Gaunt and sinewy
The threads of your once mortal muscles visible
Under your melted away skin
Declaring, to those who will listen
That you are a Child of Lucifer
Warrior of the Dark Army
Minion of Hell

But instead
You are a phantom
A neutered wraith
An entity without a home

Drifting on the wrong side of the muslin curtain
The one that demarcates the mortal world from
Wherever it is the dead dwell

You are
Utterly invisible
Screaming and ranting at a frequency that
NO ONE else can hear

It is exactly what you deserve.

O is for Owl

The roads here, in the country, are dark snake
tongues
Slippery and winding and sucking all light
I drive with both hands, clutching to see
My toddler sings to me from her car seat
And then,
BAM

An owl collides with my windshield
Making a simultaneously bell-like sound next to
A stomach-churning shattering
I hit the brakes
Bathing the bird's majestic and mortally wounded
shape
In red light
From where it has fallen into the road

When I climb out of the car to inspect it
I see that its wings are broken
And have popped free of their sockets
One pristine piece of bone protrudes
With a sickening gulp I realize
Its feathers are the same color as my daughter's hair
It is broken beyond repair
Its pupils are bobbing nonsensically in the yellow
daze of its irises

You did this. You did this. You did this.

Its chest is in its own choreography of heaving
I cover my ears and close my eyes and scream
The snake tongue road is in no way sympathetic

I climb back into the car
Turn the wheel ever so slightly
And back it up
Until I feel the telltale lump under my rear tire
I tell myself I am merciful

I can hardly wait to put the car in drive
And eliminate that ghastly red light
I know what I've done
And I drive forward, faster than I should
Heading home to pizza and electricity and sleep
And the hum drum routine of a thoroughly
unexamined life
A place absent of beating wings
And suffocating hearts
And the crunch of hollow bird bones

The next morning
And the one after that
And the one after that
My daughter points to an empty corner of the house
"Owl! Owl! Owl!"
And she hoots
Engaging in a game of call-and-response
With a saffron-eyed bird that I cannot see
But I imagine that its chest is rich with ermine
And I know that it is the perfect predator because
It doesn't need to breathe or eat or shit
It just has to hunt

"Hoo! Hoo! Hoo!" she calls
It responds at a frequency only she can hear
As it turns its head

Scanning, fluffing, blinking….

And waiting.

P is for Pine Trees

The pine trees encircle this town

Etching their shapes in the sky

Like readied weapons

Sharp and jagged, prepared to slice

They are the silent witnesses

To all of our dark deeds

Shakespearian in scope

Watching, always watching

Making us feel falsely safe

With their distance and size and stillness

They prepare all the time

Growing, standing tall to cast long shadows

Branches like fingertips reaching further into town

With each passing day

Hoping to snag and catch us

To punish us for the darkness in our heads

And the badness in our bodies

For now,

They sway innocuously

But their time will come

And ours will end

We will be

Cut to ribbons and scattered over this land

That will forget us so quickly....

And the trees will remain.

Q is for Quickly, Quietly

Quickly, quietly

      She rouses me from my flower-coated sleep.
She shouldn't be here. She isn't real.
      "I'm both," she says.

Quickly, quietly

      A translucent hand covers my mouth, icy
with the frozen water that runs through its
veins instead of blood. The temperature of
liquid death. My mouth and throat are too
cold to scream.

Quickly, quietly

      She yanks me from my bed and the grass is
too fresh and soft like baby fingers under my
feet. My nightgown whispers a warning to
my ankles, but all I can feel is the tickle of
its lacy hem

Quickly, quietly

      She tells me her story without speaking,
leading me through the thick forest without a

hiccup or tangle or misstep as her feet fall
exactly as they should with mine following
right behind and the leaves seem to glow
next to her, and they are scaly, like skin
covering the monstrous hands of the
branches

Quickly, quietly

We walk to the part of the lake that is thick
with the reeds that collect foamy detritus—
pollution, fish carcasses, leftover movement
from the waves—and they wear the filth like
pearls. The smell paints shades of blue and
green and brown inside of my nostrils. My
tongue curls as the stench hits the back of
my throat

Quickly, quietly

She tells me how her story ended right here,
after having been led there just as she led
me. The reeds were the garrote and the trees
sheltering the shoreline absorbed her
screams. Trees are excellent secret keepers.
Fatally so.

Quickly, quietly

She tells me to lean forward so she can show
me where her final gasps let in the water and
her bursting lungs made a crown of bubbles
over her head

Quickly, quietly

I slip beneath the surface, and the water's
fragile membrane, which is strong enough to
almost lovingly cup the feet of insects,
bursts for me. Water will always overpower
air, and it does for me. Soon my veins are
pumping icy water, just like hers did. Just
like they still do. I'm just like her.

Quickly, quietly

She slips into vapor and together we are all
three forms of water at once. I don't even
scream. And no one else sees her.

My story becomes water that moves and
flows and drowns things simply because
that's what it does and it doesn't know any
better.

And everything is hazy blue and silver and
bright green and the watercolor of my death
is beautiful, really. Many are not so lucky to
die in such loveliness.

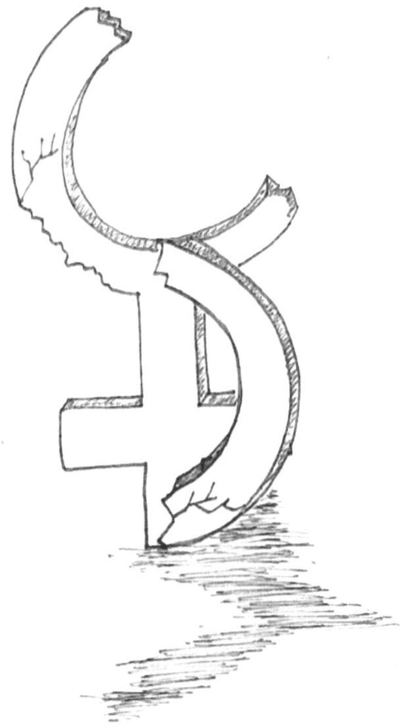

What happens to a woman when her rights are
stripped from her,
Irrevocably and unceremoniously?

What happens to her skin when it is
Rubbed raw by a cheese grater
Of legal decisions
Made by others whose bodies are not hers?
The flecks of her skin peep briefly through
The grater's metal holes
Glinting for a moment before falling
And becoming dust

Does she wait until the first pale pink drops of
blood
Begin to surface until she asks it to stop?

Or does she let the grater continue
Slowly peeling off layer after layer
Stripping off the hair and the fat and the superficial
vessels
Until reaching the arcing fibers of muscle?

Even then, does she say nothing
Until this mechanized metal of motion beyond her
control
Reaches bone?

What then?

Does she shriek and scream and cry and harden all
of the soft places within her

Striking and striking and striking again until the
grater ceases its feast?

Or does she simply pass out from the pain
And remain silent
While the mites and worms and insects
Feast on the debris
Created by her skin and tissue and her utter
existence
That has flaked off of her and landed at her feet?

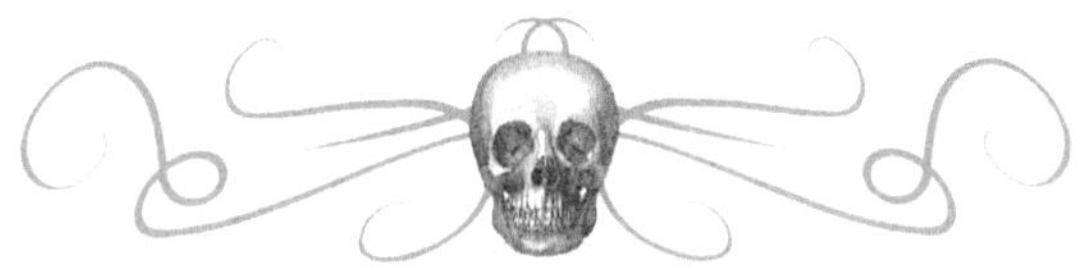

S is for Samhain (Halloween)

The grays of smoke and sky

Coat the air that is already heavy with spirit and
impending rain

Tree branches like lungs breathe it all in

And then turn crispy with rot

In a glorious display

Here we are

For such a short time

Our now-firm, calcified bones

Will crumble into dust

And our souls will dance

Unfettered by skeletal cages, especially on this day

Light and dark mingle in an energetic slurry

Blood, bone, brain, spirit smear themselves

Across the world

Today the dead come back to us

Holding our hands so thick with flesh

That we cannot feel them grasping us
82

But they're here

T is for The Town That Eats Its Young (For Trinity, Kiely, Lilly….and so many others)

It makes sense that this town should devour its
young
          The girls in particular
The ones with the tender, flaxen hair and the teeth
that are too big for their smiles
Because their faces are too young to have finished
growing
          And they're so, so young
Here, at night, the darkness is ubiquitous,
suffocating
Deadening the little licks of neon light that the
windows in town display as a hopeless torch
The throats of mine shafts open in a moan as the
wind slips through them
Giving a temporary, haunted voice to the bodies
they have digested
And the ground itself is a rolling, hungry thing
Shifting in its own murderous plate tectonics
Making footsteps unstable, orchestrating falls,
heaving the living
Into the victimhood of inertia
Letting physics do the work of death
Even conspiring with water to open up its outlaw
claws
And slip someone into a circumstance that appears
careless
          An accident
She shouldn't have let
The butterfly wings of her ribs
Open underwater

The gold here beckons
From beneath the dirt like a lady of the night

Slipping a silk stocking over eyes watery with lust,
with greed
The gold twinkles in the filth, refracting reason and
morality
A voracious rage runs under this town like quartz
veins
And we pick at it with our sickle-shaped regrets
Marveling at how quickly flesh becomes
inconsequential once it is lost

The ground here glows with the bones of these
offerings,
          These girls
Who are the fodder for the gold
Who replenish the land in its invisible bargain
Who pay the price for these riches
That require the earth to crack open and sigh and
grumble in its disruption

And its disruption turns punitive
And the gold grows
And the girls die
And their mysterious legacies snake through this
town
          Like those damned quartz veins
The color of scattered, wayward bones
Slowly disintegrating in the hostile ground

U is for Uterus

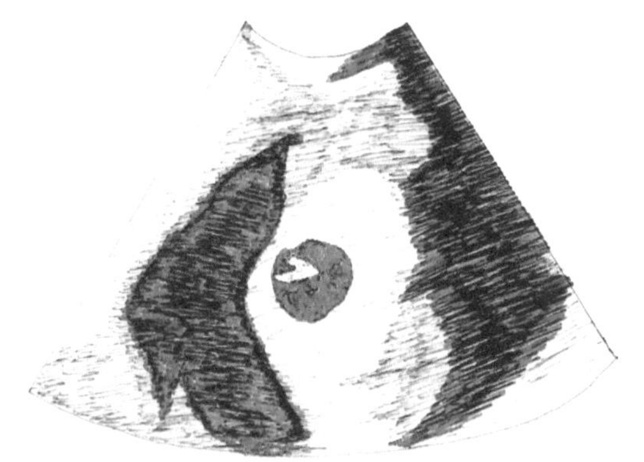

The doctor tells me,
"We need to check for stalactites in your uterus"

Bits of unwanted tissue that could create obstacles
For eyeless sperm
Trying to feel their way around in the dark

And so the doctor goes spelunking in my lady parts
Headlamp and all
Raising the caverns of that rocky dark
With injections of water
Painfully bulging the suddenly soft tissue
And I worry for a moment
That the water—necessary for exploration—
Will cause everything to calcify and harden again

I wince, and the doctor forges ahead
Walking her fingers all through that cave
Trying to leave no trace, but footprints—and
fingerprints—
Always leave a mark on delicate, natural walls

I fold my lips and bite them
Wondering if she'll find traces
Of the other two previous inhabitants of my uterus:

The child I didn't want and so another doctor
Flushed it out of my system
In a storm of fluids and blood and choice

And the child I **did** want
Who jettisoned itself out of me with such suicidal
violence

That I was certain that the cave collapsed behind it

The doctor finds nothing.
They were pieces of tissue, no heartbeat,
No consciousness, no soul
Just mucus-y deposits on the walls
There one moment and gone the next
Inconsequential

The doctor retreats from the cave
Shrugging
With no immediate explanation about
Why it is inhospitable

I thank her
And
Upon standing
The water the water the water
That she has sent up there
Gushes, splashes, pours from between my legs

And my womb is empty of
Footprints fingerprints carcasses

And once again
It is simply soft and ready….

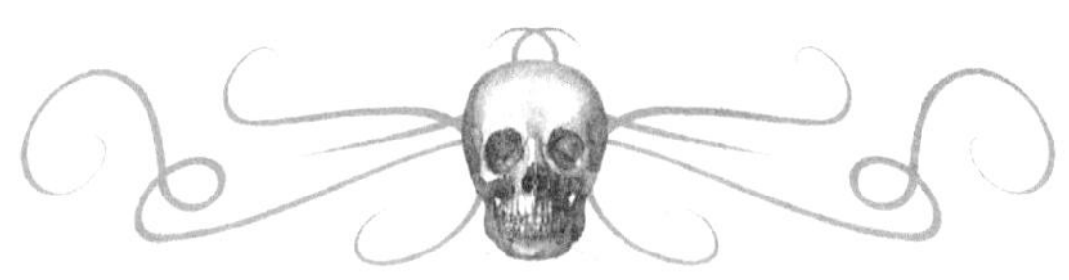

V is for Virus (COVID)

This virus
Is putrid green like the product of its coughs
It settles into muscles and fibers
Transforming cells into ball bearings
That become ignited
Producing a particular kind of aching heat just
below the surface of the skin
Thinning it like paper until
It can no longer contain the body's heavy innards
And so they crash with a jarring, clattering sound
A thousand metal marbles scattering across the floor

This virus
Sequesters and isolates, driving us into the primal
black caves
Of our human origins
As we scan the horizon for lurking danger
Except we, the infected, are the dangerous ones
Our breath and kisses and embraces are tainted
With the neon shape of illness
And the phantom wisps of contagion
Seep everywhere endlessly

This virus
Is a nightmarish carnival game:
Step right up!
Round and round this virus goes
And where it stops, nobody knows!
Will it land on a sniffle?
Or on temporarily deadened taste buds?
Or will it be a deluge of liquid death filling the
lungs?
Try your luck!

This virus
Is a dragon
And it circles the mind and body relentlessly
Scorching any hope of productivity or presence

This virus
Bullies, distorts, and manipulates

It is
A tiny little dictator
A bleary-eyed madman
An actual evil.

W is for Water

When we submerge ourselves in water
It takes on our toxins
Our stinging pain
The scaly ghosts of our fears
And it brings us relief
Buoyancy
And, when we are below the surface,
A badly needed break for our ears
And the shards of sound that stab at them ad
nauseum

But those parts of us do not get washed away
Not entirely
Nothing ever truly dissolves
The water holds everything, binding all to its
molecules
As they cycle through rivers or
Underground or
Through the copper bellies of pipes
And then back into us all over again
As we drink and bathe and
Once again seek out water as we
Command it to heal us
Transferring our stink into it

Rainwater contains pieces of corpses
The watery grave of drowned souls evaporates
And dissipates
And then precipitates
Wetting us with death
Filling streams and rivers with the
Bits of matter and energy that were left behind
when

A gasping gulp of water was a final breath
Rushing into desperate lungs and
Making them burst wide open

The drowned don't just disappear.
Water is a lockbox of our secrets
And our sins
And our pain
And our suffering.

It never, ever forgets.

X is for X-GF (Ex-Girlfriend)

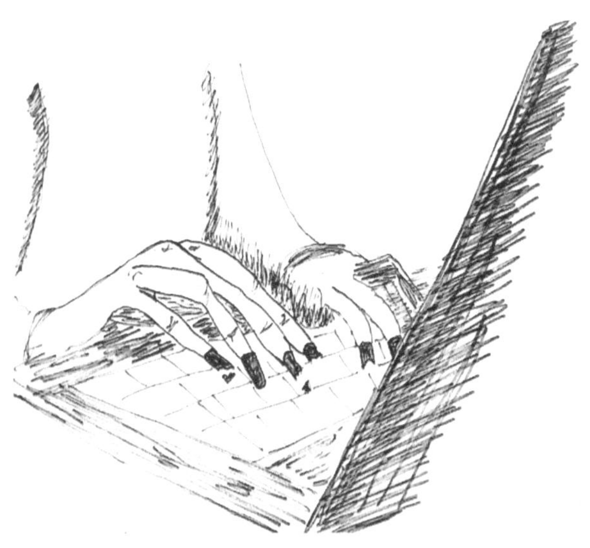

You are pervasive

Like radio waves

Unseen but certainly heard

Ranging from static to screeching to demure tunes

Circling around the one

Who slid through your dramatic manicure

The one who now belongs to me

But your nails

Can't hide the sausage-like constitution of your
fingers

In their thickness and greasiness

The skin threatens to pop each time

You bend your knuckles as you

Feverishly type

Comment after comment after comment

Longing lamentations from your social media
balcony

You have found a way to

Softly insinuate yourself into the mechanized
whirring of his life

A life that has managed to build up scope and
momentum without you

Every time he turns around

There you are

With a hair flip and teeth turned a freaky shade of
white

Even now,

When I thought I buried you too far below the
surface

To ever be seen again,

I can hear the tap tap tapping of those manicured
fingernails

Against the coffin roof

And the tapping turns to scratching

And the scratching turns to clawing

As you dig your way back up

Inhaling dirt and worms

Your eyes pulsating with the lack of oxygen.

Oh, look. You're back. Again.

Y is for Yeller

Your yelling is like

Metal spikes on the bottom of combat boots
Scraping pavement in an attempt to be cool
Your insufferable maw creates a sucking wound
In the atmosphere

Your voice is like

A small rodent being scrubbed against a washboard
Changing pitch as its skin is stripped from its bones

You yell like

You should be on a corner
Letting your nonsensical staccato tones mingle with
Traffic lights and the glazed eyes of
Apathetic, overwhelmed strangers

You yell because

Nothing is ever enough
And your mouth is constantly open in a
Sweeping movement of simultaneous starvation and
Gluttony as you
Shovel your needs into the endlessly acidic cavern
of your gut

You have a voice like

Broken door hinges, like
Microphone feedback, like
Out of tune ambulances

Your voice

Penetrates walls
Thunders down hallways
Screeches from everyone's pocket like an amber
alert
The entire tristate area is aware of your grievances
As you splatter them across everyone's ear drums

Your yelling gives me

Wrinkles across my forehead and in the back of my
throat
In the space where I swallow my tongue

Your yelling is

A scorpion sting
An ill-intentioned 747
A faulty brake
And it will drag you,
Careening,
Still yelling,
Over a cliff.

Z is for Zenith (Conclusion)

This last poem is hard to write
In the same way that goodbyes are hard to say

The words resist the page…

This book has allowed me to weave my
Fears and anger and irreverence
Through my fingers and pull on their strings
Tangling, untangling
Dangling
Mangling

We can't let the dark ugly scary things
Just stay inside of us
We must
Scream them, bleed them, cast them across
dimensions

There is boundless space and time ready to receive
them

The Universe is an unhemmed garment
Asking for us to shape it with our human
needlework
The veiny threads of our impossibly unique stories

Let this book be an invitation
Providing a weightless space for your own density
Your own tragedy
And your own levity

This book was a balm for my deeply fried
Nerves and skin and hair and thoughts

This book deconstructed my fears
And in doing so…

Reconstructed my life

Brooke MacKenzie is the author of the short fiction collection GHOST GAMES, which Kirkus Reviews called, "[a]n indelible batch of nightmarish tales." Her short fiction, poetry, and essays have been published in numerous magazines and anthologies, and she has been known to win the occasional horror writing contest. Two of her horror stories have been produced as podcast episodes by The Night's End Podcast. She grew up in a haunted house, and there is nothing she loves more than a good ghost story. Brooke has a B.A. from Sarah Lawrence College and a Ed.M. from the Harvard Graduate School of Education. She currently lives in a delightfully haunted town in Northern California with her husband and daughter.

Instagram: @mackbrookepro
Website: www.bamackenzie.com

Branigan Reed is a teaching artist, performer & all around rock-star. She spends her time trying to make the world a better place by helping people see the beauty they possess within themselves, then encouraging them to let it shine. She also sings a lot of Karaoke and reads a ton of books. Branigan lives in Salem, MA with her family, and fellow witchy-folk

Instagram: @braniganreed

May the sun shine upon you.
May all love surround you.
May the light within you, guide your way home.

Cover design by Edward Velendria
(getevel@gmail.com) | Velandria.com